Daze in the Bush

My days in the South African Bushveld

Robert V Lund

DEDICATION

To all those who dedicate their lives to the preservation of wildlife worldwide.

To all those who love and appreciate the wonderful creatures on this planet. Let us never again see a species going extinct. May our grandchildren continue to enjoy the wild splendours of the earth.

To Bunny Fineberg, second-cousin and oldest friend, who features in this book.

In memory of Walter Broeders, who shared some of these adventures with us, and whose existence on this plane ended too soon.

CONTENTS

iv

1 Introduction

I'm sure that everyone sometimes experiences something that triggers a memory of their past. One of these triggers recently got me thinking about some of the things I experienced when I was young. Specifically, I recalled my days spent in the South African bushveld. I remembered that those were exciting days for me and, I know, for my companions at the time. I realised that there was a lot that I had forgotten over time. Being age 69 now, I put my mind to work on recalling more of those times, which was, at this time, about 54 years ago. As I worked at this task, I decided to write them down so as not to lose them, and perhaps to share them with friends and family, and any other interested parties. As an already published author, I thought that there may be a chance for a book but I wasn't sure if I had enough material. I called on one of my companions of the time, Bunny, to see if he could add to the memories that I had recalled. Unfortunately, the other companion, Wally, who had shared those activities and adventures, had passed away.

2 City boys

I grew up in Johannesburg, a city much like Toronto in Canada, where I live now. Johannesburg (Joburg, for short) is part of a large metropolitan area called the Witwatersrand (an Afrikaans word for Ridge of White Waters), which is much like the GTA, or Greater Toronto Area. Joburg is far from the African bush, around 400 or so Kilometers.

I tell you this because, unless you are familiar with South Africa, you may have the mistaken notion that all of South Africa is wild with game running around all over the place. I know that some people do have that impression, amusingly demonstrated by a pair of tourists arriving at Johannesburg's Jan Smuts airport clad in khaki clothes, boots and pith helmets, ready, apparently, for the start of a safari as soon as they stepped off the plane.

Growing up, I was a city boy and totally ignorant of the really wild areas called the bushveld. And, I wasn't really interested anyway. I guess I hadn't really thought about it. Sure, I'd watched Tarzan movies and serials but those were set in the jungle and since there was nothing like that in South Africa, I couldn't relate to it. Until the age of sixteen, my only exposure to African wildlife had been at zoos. This all changed very suddenly after I had read the book *"Jock Of The Bushveld"* by Sir James Percy Fitzpatrick. If you haven't read the book or seen the fairly decent movies they made, this was the real life adventures of Fitzpatrick in a time when men could hunt for a living, and travelled by horse or ox-wagon. I will refer more to this later. By the way, the American version of the movie changed the story to give it a happier ending. The story is set in what is called the Lowveld. Just so you know, Joburg is situated in the Highveld, a geographical region in the northern part of South Africa and is about 5,500 feet above sea level. By contrast, the Lowveld lies about 300 feet above sea level. The two regions are divided by the Escarpment, which is really the northern end of the Drakensberg, a mountain range spanning almost the entire length of the country.

The two regions differ not only in altitude but also climate, temperature, and flora. The Highveld is plains-like grasslands, whereas the Lowveld is typically covered in bushes or low flat-topped acacia trees interspersed with mopane and marula trees. I think that this is the reason why the Lowveld is less populated and, therefore, has more wildlife. The Lowveld is also commonly called the Bushveld.

(See diagram)

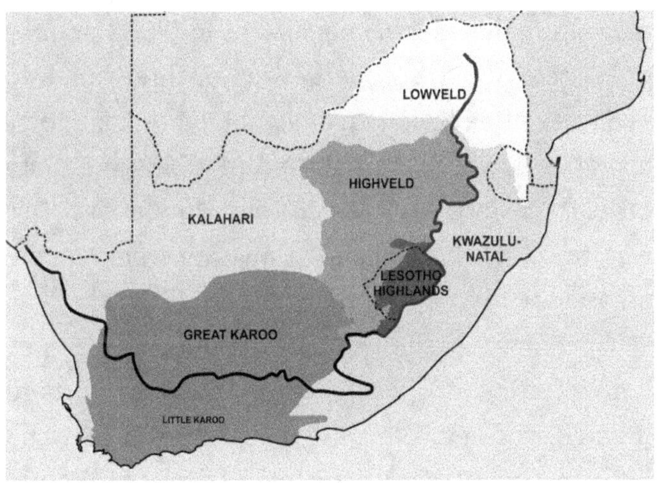

The Kruger National Park is situated in the Lowveld. You may have heard of this park, one of the largest game parks in Africa, stretching 360 Km north to south and 65 Km west to east. It is the size of England.

My "uncle" Rupert used to go hunting in the Lowveld occasionally with his father. I didn't know that at the time. I only found out when he told us that his father had just acquired a piece of property opposite the Timbavati Game Reserve and he would be going hunting more often, as a result. It was adjacent to a property owned by Ben Schoeman, who was the Minister of Transport at that time. The size of the property was four hundred Morgen. Morgen is a South African unit of land measurement, roughly equivalent to 0.86 Hectares or 2.1 acres. So the property size was three hundred and forty three hectares, or eight hundred and forty eight acres. We were also told that all the private properties were not allowed to put up fences. This was to allow the wildlife to migrate freely in the area.

Of course, we showed a lot of interest. The "we" I'm referring to was Walter (Wally), Bernard (Bunny), and me. We were all close to Rupert and his wife, Gwen. We spent a lot of time at his house.

The three of us (I'll refer to us as the Trio) were friends. Bunny is my second-cousin, Wally lived around the corner from, and we were all members of the Land Cadet marching band.

We obviously must have shown so much interest that Uncle Rupert invited the three of us to join him for a weekend at Fife, which is what the property was being called. We were so thrilled at the prospect. Of course, I had to get permission from my father first. By the way, Uncle Rupert was not an actual relative. It was a tradition in South Africa to call older people either "sir" or "uncle". That could be confusing to foreign visitors. He was pretty much like a godfather to me. Since Rupert was my dad's best friend at the time, he had no trouble convincing my father to let me go along.

The days dragged by. Fortunately, we had some excitement in the meantime. Rupert took us for some shooting practice. We went down to one of the mine dumps in the George Goch area. For those not familiar with what a mine dump in Joburg is, let me describe one. This is a huge pile of the leftover yellow soil after gold ore extraction. They were more than a hundred feet high and several hundred feet long and wide. As children, we often played on them and around them, and used to slide down the steep sides on a piece of cardboard at breathtaking speeds. It was dangerous being on them. In fact there were a number tragic accidents where children were buried when sand collapsed on them. Of course, that never deterred us. Getting back on topic, Rupert set up targets and we learned to shoot with his rifles. I'm having difficulty remembering exactly what they were. There was a .303 Lee Enfield carbine, an 8mm calibre rifle that was capable of bringing down an elephant, a Mauser .22, and his 9mm Parabellum handgun. It was exciting to be learning how to shoot and become familiar with the guns. And learning to clean them afterwards.

Finally, the weekend of our trip arrived. We all arrived at Rupert's house early, even before he came home from work. We helped pack the car with all the supplies and camping equipment. We, the trio, didn't have to bring much. Rupert supplied almost everything. We just had to ensure that we had sleeping bags, and snacks and cold drinks for the drive. Eventually, we were ready to leave.

We packed into Rupert's car – a Ford Corsair (later replaced by a Ford Cortina), and we were off! Three city teens off to become hunters in the wild.

3 Getting there

We drove east, not having to contend much with peak hour traffic, since Rupert lived in Kensington, one of the eastern suburbs of Joburg. Soon we were out of the urban areas and travelling along open road and countryside.

I don't remember what month it was but it must have been winter because it got dark fairly quickly. After at least an hour, we went through the towns of Witbank, Middleburg, Belfast, and the sleepy village of Machadodorp. We bypassed Nelspruit and drove down the winding mountain passes of the Escarpment to Sabie. Then on to White River, Bushbuck Ridge, Acornhoek, and Klaserie.

After about a three-hour drive, we were nearly there. Unfortunately, it being dark, we didn't get to see anything of the countryside, especially what would have been spectacular scenery down the Escarpment. We got onto a sand road after Bushbuck Ridge and finally came to the fenced off Timbavati Game Reserve on the right. Shortly after, we came to the entrance to Fife on the left. We had travelled about four hundred and fifty kilometres after about five hours of driving.

4 The First Night

Rupert turned into the access road and immediately stopped the car. He got out and opened the boot (trunk, to North Americans), asked us to get out and help him take out a rifle and a torch (flashlight to North Americans). What struck me immediately I was outside was the smell of the air – it was totally different to city air – fresh, clean, and something else I couldn't identify. Thinking back, I suspect it was the vegetation and the extra oxygen. Another thing that struck me was the quiet. No traffic sounds. It was not total silence – there was a constant hum of insects, but no other sound – so different to the city. It was also somewhat exciting, as we were out in the bush, in total darkness- with unknown creatures out there, possibly close by.

After loading the rifle, Rupert ordered us all back in the car. He gave the rifle to Wally, who was up front, and the torches (which were actually powerful spotlights) to Bunny and me, telling us to shine it out the open window and look for the reflection of eyes. We set off down the road, which was really just a set of parallel tracks in the grass, with Bunny shining the light to the left and me shining to the right. At the time, I didn't know that what we were doing was actually illegal. It was illegal because it was deemed unfair, for reasons which will become clear.

Rupert said that whoever killed an animal would get the skin. We had been driving for about five minutes when Bunny spotted eyes reflecting the light – many eyes. Rupert slowed the car and we saw that it was a herd of Impala, the most common antelope in that part of the country. They were about twenty metres away (about sixty feet), standing looking at us. Actually, they were mesmerised by the light. Rupert slowly brought to car to a stop and we exited slowly and quietly. He told Wally to shoot and to aim just below and behind the front shoulder. Wally was so excited and he was shaking so much that he couldn't aim. He passed the rifle to Bunny. Bunny tried to aim but couldn't find the target in the scope. Rupert swapped weapons with him (he was carrying the 9mm Parabellum pistol), took aim and was about to fire when the herd started bounding away. Bunny remembered a tip Rupert had given us once about antelope being brought to a halt by a whistle. He gave a high-pitched whistle and, amazingly, the herd stopped and stared our way again. Rupert took the shot and brought a female Impala down. The others streaked away and disappeared into the dark bush.

We all quickly walked over to where we had seen the animal go down. As we got closer, Rupert warned us to be wary, as a kick from the sharp hooves of an antelope could slice one open. The impala was still alive and occasionally threshing around trying to stand up. Rupert told Bunny to shoot it in the head, which he did successfully and the antelope was lifeless. We had meat! Bunny said "I'm getting the skin!" Rupert said "But I shot it!" Bunny replied "You said whoever kills it gets the skin. I killed it!" Bunny had that skin on his bedroom floor for years.

Bunny said to me "Did you see how Wally was shaking – he couldn't even shoot!" I laughed and said to him "So were you, and you were aiming all over the place!"

Rupert told us each to take a leg of the impala and we carried it back to the car. I was wondering how we were going to transport the carcass since there was no roof-rack. Rupert had obviously done this before and indicated that we sling the carcass on the bonnet of the car (trunk, to North Americans), with the legs facing back. Wally had to hold onto one set of legs through the window, while

Rupert, in the driver's seat held onto the other legs. We drove like this for another fifteen minutes, approximately, until we saw some light up ahead and finally arrived at the camp.

Apparently Rupert had invited a couple of friends to Fife and they had arrived before us. The camp was just a half-built house and a couple of rondavels (a rondavel is a round hut with a thatch roof). The light was from a couple of powerful paraffin (kerosene) lamps – there was no electricity at the camp. There was also a campfire going. After greetings, they were introduced as Groot Piet (Big Piet) and Klein Piet (Small Piet). Small? He was an enormous man. They said that they were hungry and they took the impala carcass, hung it up and gutted it. One of them then proceeded to take the liver out of the impala, smother it in salt, and threw it on a grill that covered the campfire. After about a minute, he turned it over then, after another minute removed it from the fire, proceeded to cut it into pieces and gave the first piece to Bunny. Bunny was reluctant to take it but Piet said that since he had killed it, he had to take the first bite, which he did hesitantly. Piet then proceeded to hand slices out to everyone. Now, at that time, I was not very partial to liver so I also very reluctantly accepted the piece and took a bite. Was

I ever surprised – it turned out to be so delicious that I wanted more, and so did Bunny and Wally.

After hauling out some folding chairs, we sat around the campfire and Rupert gave us each a beer. Now this may surprise you but I had never had beer before. My father drank wine, brandy, and the occasional liqueur, never beer. My first taste was not one I enjoyed. I didn't like the bitter hoppy taste (but that would soon change). I was thirsty, so I drank it.

Rupert was chatting to his friends when another man appeared out of the bush, which was rather disconcerting to me. It turned out to be the man employed to look after the property. He lived in a little hut about twenty metres away. His name was Mbilo and he was a Shangaan (a very proud indigenous tribe, prevalent in Mozambique). Rupert suggested that Mbilo take us (the trio) for a walk. I wasn't sure where we were going to walk – all I could see around us was bush - dark, dark bush. Rupert gave Wally the torch and we were on our way.

Mbilo led us on a narrow little animal trail and we had to walk in single file with Mbilo leading followed by Wally, then Bunny, then me at the rear. Within a minute, we could no longer see the light from the camp. Wally was shining the torch left and right, but when I looked left and right all I saw was an inky darkness. Mbilo, it seemed didn't need the light. He seemed to know exactly where he was going. To say I was a little apprehensive would be an understatement. What if there were lions nearby, or a leopard, or other dangerous creatures? We wouldn't even see them.

I made sure to follow Bunny closely and he was following Wally closely because without that torch we would be in almost total darkness. We had been walking for some time and my apprehension was growing – not being in control and in a very scary environment. I think Bunny was feeling it too because he said that we had walked enough, that we were tired and should start getting back to the camp. Wally communicated to Mbilo that we wanted to go back. Mbilo nodded, but kept walking on. Now we didn't know how well he understood English, so after a few minutes we again said to him that we must go back. Again he nodded but kept walking. Now we were all a little apprehensive and after a few minutes we again asked Mbilo to take us back, this time using our hands to try and explain what we wanted. "Yes, we go back" said Mbilo, but he just kept walking. I was about to grab him and turn him around and point the way back when we saw some light up ahead.

As we got closer, we could see it was a building similar to our camp. As we got closer, we saw people sitting around a campfire. As we got even closer, we saw that it was Rupert and his friends! We all laughed with relief and realized that while we thought that we were walking in a straight path, Mbilo had taken us in a big semi-circle and arrived at the camp from the opposite side. That was quite the experience but it was also our first important bush lesson.

Of course, Rupert and his friends found our ordeal rather amusing.

Sitting around the campfire, which was fed by logs of camelthorn - which had a nice fragrance, we drank more beer and chatted. Rupert shared some hunting stories which kept us fascinated. Eventually everyone declared that they were tired and it was time for bed. Asking Rupert where we (the trio) were going to sleep, he indicated one of the rondavels. We hauled our sleeping bags out of the car and went into the rondavel. It was then that we discovered that the rondavels were still under construction and that there were no doors and no windows, just gaping spaces where they would eventually be fitted. This set off alarm bells and we pointed out to Rupert that lions, leopards, hyenas, could just walk in and have an easy meal, not to mention snakes and other creatures. He just laughed and said we'd be alright.

With trepidation, we laid our sleeping bags out on the metal cots in the hut. At least we wouldn't be on the ground and have to worry about snakes crawling into our sleeping bags. The "ceiling", which was the grass thatch, was full of large moths, spiders, and some lizards. Not comforting! I changed into a track suit and, with some apprehension, got into my sleeping bag, in the dark, and tried to sleep. However, sleep would not come.

Now I could clearly hear the sounds of the bush at night - sounds foreign to me. There was the constant buzz, hum and chirping of insects, calls of frogs, cries of some birds (birds?). However, there were the occasional sounds of bigger creatures – the screech of monkeys, the bark of a baboon, the cough of an antelope, or was that a hyena, or a leopard, or a lion? Eventually, though, we all drifted off to sleep.

5 The first hunt

I woke to the aroma of cooking bacon. Putting on my shoes, after carefully checking inside them for spiders, scorpions and other nasty creepy-crawlies, I followed my nose. Klein Piet was frying bacon, eggs, sausages and tomatoes on a grill over a fire that had been made in the partially constructed house. I saw then that there were only three walls and half a roof. Rupert and friends had slept there. It was more open than the rondavels. Brave, or crazy, I thought. A few meters away, was a huge wind driven water pump. We were told later that it was the tallest in the Lowveld.

Soon everyone was up and we tucked into breakfast, mopping up the egg-yolk with bread, and followed by instant coffee with sweetened condensed milk.

After breakfast, we were ready to hit the bush. Rupert and friends decided not to hunt and Rupert asked Mbilo to take us (the trio) out and track some game. We each filled up a water canteen and strapped it to our belts, then set off on one of the animal trails.

As we walked I noticed that there were so many animal trails criss-crossing the one we were on. In the daylight, we could now see into the bush, unlike the night before. However, most of the time, one could only see about thirty metres due to the density of the trees, grass and bushes. The grass was around two to three feet high and was fairly dry, the colour of straw. Anything could hide in that grass to within a few feet. The trees were rarely more than about twelve feet high.

The sound of the bush was still very noticeable, similar to the night sound but with more birds. Especially noticeable was the constant call of turtle doves, the occasional loud squawk of Hadedah Ibis, and the distinctive song of the Piet-my-vrou (Red cuckoo with a sound similar to the whippoorwill, but ending on a lower note), and Loeries.

We walked in single file again, behind Mbilo. He paused occasionally to scan the ground and would sometimes change direction, taking a different animal trail. I presumed that he was tracking game.

After about thirty minutes, he stopped, knelt down slowly, and put his finger to his lips, indicating that we should be quiet and kneel. He pointed to the side whispering "shoot". I looked at where he was pointing but could see nothing. The others also looked and shook their heads. Mbilo said "impala, shoot", pointing again. I saw nothing but grass and bush. The others shrugged their shoulders, seeing nothing either. Just then, I saw a slight movement – an impala suddenly became visible as if it had manifested out of thin air. The others saw it too and I could see the surprise on their faces. The animals were so camouflaged that it took the flick of an ear to recognise what it was. Bunny quickly brought the rifle to his shoulder but before he could aim, the whole herd (which I hadn't noticed before) took off in leaps and bounds, startled by the movement. We were also startled to see a whole herd where we saw nothing a moment previously. Bunny never even managed to take a shot.

We walked over to where the herd had been and Mbilo had us quickly following their spoor. After about fifteen minutes, Mbilo pointed again, and knelt but the herd spooked and took off again before we could do anything. We really had to work on our stealth skills! We continued to follow the herd but never quite caught up to them again. We must have spent an hour or more tracking them. It was becoming rather hot and we decided to head back to camp. Mbilo knew the direct way but it still took more than an hour to get back.

We were pretty thirsty and tucked into the cool beers, and I found the beer strangely refreshing that time. While we drank, I enjoyed the aroma of braaied (barbequed) impala ribs that someone had put on the grill.

I had brought along a multi-purpose camping tool. It was an axe, a hammer, a crowbar, a nail remover, and a bottle opener. Mbilo said he really liked it. I decided that I would give it to him when we left as a token of my appreciation for his help.

When we did leave, I gave the tool to him. He then presented Bunny with a traditional assegai. On the way home, I expressed my surprise to Bunny that Mbilo had not given the assegai to me. Bunny laughed and told me that he had said to Mbilo that he (Bunny) would persuade me to give him the axe. So Mbilo therefore gave the gift to Bunny in gratitude. Bloody hell!

After a lunch of smoky impala ribs and a salad made of just tomato, onion, and cucumber, Rupert told us that we had some work to do. We were to butcher the impala carcass.

After taking some cuts for the rest of our meals, we sliced the meat into strips to be used for making biltong. Biltong is salted dried meat, a traditional South African snack food dating back to the time of the Voortrekkers (the Dutch pioneers who eventually became the Boers). The Americans have a similar food called jerky, which is not as nice. We had a large container (about two feet by three feet) into which we threw a layer of coarse salt. We then laid strips of meat, followed by more salt, then more meat, etc., continuing until all the meat was used up.

The biltong would be shared out and taken home and allowed to dry for a while before it was ready to consume.

The container of meat was covered and stowed away so that it could not be got at by interested wild life.

That chore done, someone made the suggestion that we climb the wind pump. We were told that it was the tallest in the Lowveld and also had the deepest borehole. I seem to recall that it was about sixty feet high. This we did and were rewarded with an amazing view. It seemed we could see forever.

The bushveld lay as far as we could see to the north and the east. To the southwest, the two thousand foot high escarpment could be seen faintly in the heat haze. To the north, we could see huge mine dumps and mineshafts and the mining town of Phalaborwa in the far distance. Below, we could see the buildings of the camp and we could also see Mbilo's hut and, next to that, a pond that had obviously been formed by water from the pump. We realized that we would probably see animals coming to drink there. We were told later that shooting anywhere within a mile of the waterhole was strictly taboo.

After descending, we realized there wouldn't be enough daylight for another hunt. However, we (the trio) took the rifles and went for a walk, without Mbilo, to familiarise ourselves with the vicinity. We knew that we wouldn't get lost because we could easily see the wind pump. The only animals we encountered were a few lizards and a little duiker which shot away very quickly. Damn, we really had to learn some stealth skills.

Returning to camp, we were again assailed by a wonderfully fragrant cooking aroma. Someone had made a curry. Thirsty, we downed a few more beers. After a delicious supper of curried impala with rice and chutney, we sat around the campfire drinking beer.

When it got dark, I looked up at the night sky and was astounded. I hadn't noticed this the night before. The Milky Way, in all its glory, stretching from horizon to horizon, with its multi-coloured clouds and bazillion stars, was a sight I had never seen before. This was not something that one saw in the city. I felt so small and insignificant looking at that awesome magnificence. I gazed in awe for a long time while waxing philosophical to myself.

After a while I turned my attention to the sounds of the bush. They were not so scary anymore. There were crickets – different kinds making slightly different sounds; there was the constant sound of cicadas; there were at least three different birds making different calls and there were birds flying overhead occasionally. I recognized the sound of kiewiets (this was the Afrikaans name for a type of Crowned Plover). There were different frog or toad calls. These must have been coming from the pond since there was no other water close by. There was the occasional bark of a jackal and the laugh of a hyena. Once, I heard the trumpeting of an elephant. Also, if one listened closely, the sound of smaller animals moving in the grass could be heard. I grew to love these sounds.

That day left us dazed and amazed.

6 Bits and pieces

We (the trio) were invited to visit Fife a few times over a period of two years and always jumped at the chance. It was always exciting getting out into the bush.

For me, many of the experiences of our time there are jumbled in my memory so I'll just relate them as I recall them.

I will also include some anecdotes relating to other visitors to Fife.

For example, one day Rupert had very bad toothache. He couldn't take the pain anymore. The nearest Dentist was very far away. He decided to do something about it. He took a piece of cloth and wrapped it around the tooth then took some pliers and worked the tooth loose before finally yanking it out. Lots of Brandy was swallowed, both before and after the extraction. Ouch!

7 Lots of misses

Obviously, we were not experienced hunters. Our many misses were testament to that. It's one thing shooting at stationary targets at a shooting range but totally different when you are out in the bush shooting at live animals, especially while trying to be stealthy.

Our first day hunt would have been an easy shot if we had seen the animals. That was a great lesson and we did eventually learn to spot camouflaged game.

On another occasion the three of us were walking along the access road when we spotted a duiker about fifteen metres away. Since the duiker is a small antelope, and Wally was carrying the .22 rifle, we silently decided that he should take the shot. We were partly behind a tree trunk and managed to not spook the animal. It was an easy shot. Wally let fly. The duiker jumped and shot away into the bushes. I was wondering how Wally could possibly have missed the shot, when a thin branch of the tree fell to the ground just in front of him. It seems that he had somehow not seen the branch (actually more like a twig) in the line of fire, and hit it which deflected the bullet. We had a good laugh at that one.

One day, we were walking along and saw a flock of guinea fowl. Now guinea fowl are good eating. They were just about ten metres away and didn't fly off when they saw us. Actually, guinea fowl are like chickens in that they don't really fly like other birds but they can flap themselves into a low tree.

We discovered that day that guinea fowl are the canniest birds on earth. Since we could not shoot them with the larger rifles (they would explode into a ball of feathers), we had to use the .22 which wouldn't do a lot of damage.

I raised the rifle to my shoulder and lined up the shot on the nearest bird. As I was about to squeeze the trigger, the bird darted into a bush. Ok, so I selected another bird, lined up the shot and started to squeeze the trigger when the bird shot into the bush. Damn. I lined up another one and I was frazzled when the same thing happened. This happened five times! Could these birds read my mind? Flummoxed, I gave up. With that kind of action, they deserved to live!

One day, we were out with a friend of Mbilo's. Mbilo had gone home to visit family in Mozambique and had his friend look after the property while he was away. I don't remember his name, so we'll call him Zonda. After walking for a couple of hours, Zonda picked up the spoor of some wildebeest and zebra. For some reason these two species always hung out together. We followed for a while and came to a place where we saw that a line of trees had been cut down. We were a bit puzzled about this but Zonda eventually made us realize that this was the border of the property. If we went further, we would be poaching on the property belonging to Ben Schoeman, the then Minister of Transport. We said we should turn back but Zonda insisted that it would be alright. He continued tracking. Eventually we came to a large clearing where we spotted four giraffe. Behind them, a little further away, were a large herd of Burchell's zebra mixed with a few dozen wildebeest (gnu).

The giraffe were about twenty-five metres away and to our surprise, they did not run away. We stood in awe of these giant gentle creatures. Only when we tried to get closer did they casually lope away with their huge swaying gait, seemingly in slow motion. We did not want to shoot the giraffe, not only because they were so majestic, but we would never have been able to get the carcass back to camp. Additionally, we did not have a licence to shoot anything but one impala (not that that would have stopped us).

We selected one wildebeest and decided all three of us would shoot at the same animal, lessening the chance of a miss. We lined up a fairly easy shot on a wildebeest slightly away from the herd. Just then, the giraffe turned and ran towards the herd, sparking a stampede. We managed to shoot before the target ran. The wildebeest jumped into the air and we thought it had definitely been hit. We were about to walk to where we thought it should be but Zonda said we missed. He then asked us if we would shoot a giraffe for him, and we were not to tell the "boss" (meaning Rupert's father). We refused. Zonda then said that we should go back now. Later, we figured that we probably didn't miss the wildebeest and that Zonda probably went back to get the carcass for himself.

The only times we didn't miss was on the nights we arrived at Fife and used the torches along the access road to the camp. This was unfair, I know, but we justified it by the fact that we were shooting for the pot.

8 Hunting a lion

We were tramping through the bush for a few hours. It was the three of us, without Mbilo. We'd grown confident enough to venture out without a guide.

We heard a roar, which quickly got the adrenalin going. Discussing what we were going to do, we all decided that we were going to bag a lion that day. Looking back on that day, later in my life, I knew that that was a bad decision — three inexperienced hunters going after a lion could have had a really bad outcome.

We couldn't see the animal, so we started moving toward where the roar had come from. Walking for a while, we still had not yet seen anything. We also had not heard any further sound. We tried to look for some spoor but found nothing. As we were discussing what to do next, the roar was repeated, coming from a different direction. It sounded fairly close by. We started walking toward the sound again.

As we walked, we intermittently heard the roar. We hadn't caught up with it yet, but we at least determined that the direction was now consistent and we were actually following the animal. We continued moving toward the sound but it never seemed to be any closer. We realised that, if we wanted to get the animal, we had to step up our pace. This required considerable effort in the heat.

After some time, the sound was becoming louder, so we knew that we were getting closer. The effort was taking its toll on us though, we were tiring. I was thinking "damn this lion. It was moving pretty fast for an animal that normally sleeps during the day." Since we were getting closer, we continued on, even though our enthusiasm was waning.

The latest roar indicated that we were very close now, but we still couldn't see the animal. Bear in mind that, in this bush, one couldn't see more than about twenty to thirty metres. Then we got lucky – we came across a clearing that was about ten metres wide and about fifty metres long and there, at the far side we, at last, saw the source of the roars that we had been following.

To our big surprise, though, we saw that what we had been tracking was not a lion at all but a large kudu bull. This was the source of the roar that we heard. We were so flabbergasted that we laughed, which, of course scared the kudu, which went charging away before we could even think of shooting. Another missed opportunity. That would have delivered a lot of meat!

We were now so bushed (excuse the pun) that we decided to head back to camp. However, that would be the start of another adventure, and a good lesson about the bush.

9 Going in circles

We wanted to get back to camp to have a shower and down a few beers. However, following the "lion" had disoriented us – we didn't know which way would take us back. No problem though, we thought, we just had to look for the wind pump, which could be seen from far away. However, we couldn't see it due to the thickness of the trees and bushes. Fortunately, we spotted an anthill close by which was about two metres high. Climbing that,

Bunny spotted the top of the wind-pump. Being in a clearing helped.

We set off in its direction, figuring about a forty-five minute walk. After about thirty minutes, we decided to check that we were still heading in the right direction. We looked for another anthill, of which there were plenty. Climbing up, I had a look around but couldn't see it. The bushes and trees were too close and we couldn't see another clearing. Wally decided to climb a tree, which gave him a better view over the bush. However, he couldn't see the wind-pump ahead. Turning around, he spotted it – behind us, and it was still quite far away! So we took off in that direction and after about fifteen minutes, we decided to check our heading again. Climbing another tree (and I must tell you that it was not easy getting up those trees, especially trying to avoid the very nasty three-inch long thorns), I saw the wind-pump to the left of our heading, and still quite far away. This was very disconcerting.

We headed off in that direction, this time checking our bearings every few minutes. We were always off-course but eventually made it, trudging into camp exhausted from the heat and effort. We sank into chairs and downed quite a few beers before getting enough energy to take a shower at the wind-pump. There being no electricity, there was no hot water, but the cold water was very refreshing.

So the practical lesson we learned that day was that, because one cannot walk in a straight line in the bush, every slight deviation made one eventually walk in a circular route. This is something that I should have known, having read of the phenomena in *Jock Of The Bushveld*. Anyway, we were prepared for future treks in the bush.

I was grateful for the wind-pump, both for the cool shower and for showing us the way back.

10 The "Leopard"

During the day, we drank a lot of beer (of which there was always a plentiful supply). We could easily consume more than a dozen beers with no effects (for fifteen year olds that was quite something). I imagine that all the walking in the heat had something to do with it.

At night, it was a different story. Maybe because it was slightly cooler and we weren't spending energy walking. Maybe it was a cumulative effect. I don't know. Regardless, everyone in the camp would become a little tipsy. Especially when we were also downing Rupert's father's home-made plum wine.

We were first introduced his plum wine when he gave a shovel to Bunny and told him to follow. At a certain spot, he told Bunny to dig, and to dig slowly and carefully. Hitting something that sounded like glass, the digging continued by hand. Shortly after, a large glass jar was unearthed. This was where Rupert's father aged his plum wine.

The morning after the first time downing that stuff, I was found with just my head on the cot, and Wally was on the floor – he didn't make it to his sleeping bag either. Startlingly, there were hyena paw prints in the dust all around the rondavel floor. I guess they weren't hungry that night. Man, that stuff tasted nice, like more!

So you will understand why the following incident occured.

Everyone was seated around the campfire, talking, drinking, and laughing when someone shouted "Oh crap, there's a leopard!" Looking around, I couldn't see any leopard and neither could the others. "Where? Where?" some of us shouted. "Up in the tree!" He pointed. We looked and saw these two reflected orbs fairly high in the tree. Someone grabbed a rifle, took aim, and fired. Nothing happened. No movement. Another shot was taken, with no change. Then someone laughed and said it wasn't a leopard, it was a giraffe. Another shot was taken, with still no movement. By now, someone's brain had surfaced through the alcoholic haze – they shone a torch up into the tree to see just what it was.

It turned out to be two beer cans that someone had thrown into the tree at some time. They had landed with the concave bottoms pointing towards the camp providing a good reflection of the lamp, looking like animal eyes.

11 A Donkey Is No Ass

At a time in my life when I was doing a lot of discovery, I learned that donkeys are as lazy as most people believe them to be, but not as stupid as some people think they are. In fact, I discovered that they will deliberately think of ways to get out of doing work.

Mbilo owned a few donkeys that he kept around his hut. They were not fenced in and were free to roam around during the day.

On one of our visits, we decided that we were going to ride these donkeys (there were no horses on the "farm"). Mbilo had told Bunny to be careful with the small donkey because it would often buck its rider. Bunny told me what Mbilo had said. However, he told Wally that it was the big one that bucked.

So, having carefully selected my steed (the big one), I stroked its head, and then hopped on his back. Having no saddle and stirrups, I grabbed hold of its mane, or whatever you call the hair down a donkey's neck, and prepared for the ride of my life. I tapped my heels into its ribs, the way they do in the Western movies, made the right clicking noise and was ready to go flying down the road. Only....nothing happened, the donkey just stood there. I jabbed my heels in a bit harder but to no avail. I thrust forward to try to indicate that I was after some movement, but got no response.

We had made sure that Wally got the small donkey. His mounted it, but his "steed" was motionless too. Bunny decided to help (I'm not sure that "help" is the right word here) by slapping Wally's ride on the rump. That certainly worked and the donkey, true to its reputation threw Wally into the air, vertically. As Wally landed back on its back, it took off like a shot. Wally, who was unprepared for the sudden movement, did a backflip somersault in place and landed on his butt on the ground.

I was laughing so much that I didn't see Bunny move behind me and slap the butt of my donkey. It shot off and, catching me unawares, I wasn't holding on, so I also did a back flip and landed on my butt in the dirt. I wasn't laughing any more, but both Bunny and Wally were, hysterically.

Not discouraged, and now understanding the means of motivating these animals into movement, I broke a branch off of a tree, making a little switch, like professional jockeys use. Back on the donkey, I used the branch to lightly whack the donkey's rump. I didn't really expect it to work so, of course, I wasn't holding on when the donkey took off like a rocket, and landed on my butt once more. Fortunately, the donkey, having shed its load, came to a stop.

Now I had the secret, I was eager to try again. As I lifted my leg over the donkey however, it decided to take one step away. Undaunted, I took another step closer and prepared to mount again, but the donkey went another step too. I tried again: same thing. Then I saw the donkey giving me a sideways glance, and I knew then that he was toying with me. Determined, though, I took two quick steps, surprising the creature, and managed to hop on. Even though I couldn't see his face now, I could sense the donkey's consternation. My smirk however did not last long.

This time, holding on, I applied the stick as before, but nothing happened. I applied the switch a bit more forcibly, but he wasn't budging. Repeated whacking produced no results. So then I tried a new approach: I pushed the stick under his tail and prodded the donkey's more sensitive areas. This got him going and off we went. However, we were not going down the road, as I had anticipated, we were moving towards the fence. This is definitely not where I wanted to go, as it was a barbed wire fence. At that point in time, I realized that I had nothing to steer the donkey with, and pulling on his mane didn't produced the desired effect.

When we got close to the fence, the donkey then turned parallel to the fence and started moving closer. I realized, then, that this creature was out to get me, and I had to jump off to avoid getting my legs ripped to shreds on the barbed wire. Strangely, the others were having the same experience. After that, we decided to give up.

Long afterwards, it dawned on me that this creature had the same philosophy as me at that time: the only thing worth putting effort into was finding ways to get out of doing any work. Much later on, I learnt from this that determination could only get you so far and no further, without cooperation.

I've learned and experienced, over the years, that animals have much more intelligence, and emotions, than most humans give them credit for. This is something to bear in mind when dealing with all animals.

12 Alone

There came a time when the three of us didn't always go out into the bush together. Sometimes it would be just two of us, and sometimes we would go out alone, if no one else was up to it.

One afternoon, after lunch, it was very hot and no one else felt like tramping around in the heat (sometimes the summer temperatures reached over forty degrees Celsius). I decided to go out on my own. I loved being out in the bush. I walked for a while but soon got hot. I found a shady tree and sat down, leaning against its trunk. Next to the tree was a dry stream bed. This was interesting because I had never seen running water on the property. I wondered when it last had water running in it.

That day, I came to realise that we were always so focused on searching for game that we had been missing a whole universe of other life.

I sat there looking at all sorts of amazing birds in the trees and on the ground (catching insects). There were many very colourful birds that I had never seen before. I also spotted a large hornbill.

Looking at the ground, I saw different types and sizes of ants, from tiny ones about two millimetres long to large black ants about an inch long. There were red ants too with mean looking pincers. I saw different types of beetles. They differed in size from a few millimetres to large dung beetles about an inch and a half in size. Most of them were black, but there were colourful ones too. Some were striped and some were spotted, including ladybugs. I saw cicadas on the trees, singing away with their shrill call. There were lizards. Again, from small to larger, some striped, some plain.

I saw flies, types of which I had never seen before. There were small ones with weird-shaped wings, others similar to house flies, and large shiny greenbottles.

I saw a few different species of dragonflies, some plain, some colourful. I caught sight of a green praying mantis.

On the ground were the tiniest flowers I had ever seen. I had to look up close to see them. There were a few different types, existing somehow in the dry dusty soil. They could not be seen when standing up.

I was fascinated, mesmerised, at this amazing micro world that we had totally overlooked. Sitting, leaning against the tree, I felt at peace with the world.

Then, the most amazing thing happened. Out of the corner of my eye, I saw movement, something larger. I froze at first then turned my head very slowly to try and see what it was. Walking into my view was a bushbuck. It didn't see me and wasn't in an alert state - it was like I was invisible. It was a young one with small horns, only just beginning to twist. It was smaller than an adult impala. I thought it was beautiful, and I felt no desire to shoot it. It walked slowly past me about four metres away. I exclaimed a silent "wow".

Eventually, I dragged myself away and walked back to camp feeling very much content and at peace with the world.

13 The Cat

I was not present at Fife when the following incident took place. It was one of the campfire stories told to us by Rupert.

Rupert's wife, Gwen, was never interested in coming out to Fife. She preferred the comfort of home. However, Rupert managed to persuade her to spend a weekend on the property. However, she didn't want to leave the cat alone at home for that long. She decided to bring the cat along on the trip.

At that stage, before the new house was being built at the camp, there was a little one-room cottage made of wood and corrugated iron sheets, with wooden window shutters.

The first night and next day passed without incident. However, on the second night, in the early hours of the morning, the cat was clawing at the door, wanting to be let out, waking them both.

The cat was let out. About a minute later, there was a deep roar, unmistakably from a lion, and a loud squeal from the cat, then silence. I'm going to leave the rest to your imagination.

Gwen never went back to Fife again.

14 Near Miss, Fortunately

As I mentioned before, there were times when we (the trio) did not always go out together. On one occasion, Bunny and I decided to see what we could find. Wally said he may go out later.

We were walking, doing the usual thing, looking for game. We had by this time learned a bit about tracking and reading spoor. We could identify many different types of animal from their tracks, and from their droppings.

We were putting some of that knowledge into practice, and were on the trail of some impala.
After a while, we heard the sound of something moving through the bush, coming our way. We froze, waiting see what it was. Suddenly, we heard a shot and the sound of a bullet from a rifle that went streaking by us, very, very close. Before we could react, there was the sound of something large crashing through the brush towards us. Coming into view, we saw that it was Wally. When he saw us, his eyes went wide and his mouth hung open. I think we had the same expression. After the initial shock, we swore at him and shouted "Are you crazy? You nearly killed us! What the hell did you think you were doing?" (but in much less polite language). After apologising profusely, he said that he saw movement through the bush and thought he was shooting at an animal.

That was another miss but it was a fortunate miss. That could have been a tragic incident.

It was also another lesson learned – never shoot at anything unless you've identified the target.

15 Alcoholic Elephants

Mbilo lived in his little hut adjacent to the campsite. He had only a bicycle for transport. While Rupert's father would always bring basic supplies whenever he came to Fife, there were always the little extras he wanted. Unfortunately, the nearest store was dozens of kilometres away.

Obtaining alcoholic drinks was always a problem as the nearest store didn't sell any. So Mbilo did what most rural dwelling Africans did: he made his own. His most common brew was sorghum beer.

Sorghum, if you don't know, is a grain and in South Africa is used for making porridge (Maltabela was my favorite – delicious) and what was commonly called Bantu Beer. This is what Mbilo often made.

Occasionally, however, when it was in season, the Marula tree would produce a delicious sweet fruit. Many animals in the bush would eat the fruit fallen to the ground. Birds, Elephants, monkeys, baboons, and antelope loved it. In a bumper season, there would be more fruit than could be eaten and the marula "berries" would lie on the ground for many days. Due to the high sugar content, they would eventually ferment and turn alcoholic. The animals would still eat them in this state and, as a result (and you may find this hard to believe but it's true), they would get drunk.

I have not witnessed this phenomenon in the wild but I have seen documentary videos of it. It is most amusing. The animals would behave crazily, especially the monkeys and baboons. Warthogs, giraffe, elephants and ostriches would stagger around. Baboons would act wildly, often doing somersaults.

The next day there would be hangovers. It's actually funny to see a baboon holding his hand to his forehead and groaning, just like humans.

So, when the season arrived, Mbilo would gather marula fruit and make a fermented alcoholic drink out of them. In fact, he would make a lot – as much as he could store. He would store the brew in paraffin tins (one gallon kerosene cans) with screw-top plugs and stack them in his hut.

One season, when his hut was still a wood and corrugated iron construction, he had stored a lot of the brew inside. He must have messed a little, leaving an aroma that wafted into the bush. That aroma attracted some unwanted attention. A small herd of elephants found the aroma very tantalising and wanted to get at the source. This they did and flattened Mbilo's hut in the process. It was totally destroyed.

Rupert's father arranged for a sturdier cinder block hut to be built for Mbilo. I'm not sure where he stored his brew after that incident.

16 The Buffalo

Tom was a friend of Rupert's. He was also friends with my dad. I met him when he helped my father to silver a mirror lens for a ten-inch reflecting telescope that my dad was building. It was an amazing telescope. Tom was well respected in the academic scientific community.
He would occasionally visit Fife to spend a weekend with Rupert. However, he seemed to have some bad luck relating to those visits.

On one occasion, he had fallen asleep behind the wheel of his car on the way to Fife resulting in the car flipping and him being severely injured. He had some broken bones and was also scalped in the accident.

On one of his visits to Fife, he had gone off into the bush on his own. He came across a small herd of Cape Buffalo. He selected one, aimed and fired. He heard the slap of the bullet hitting muscle. The herd scattered, of course, but his target had not gone down. It was a rule that one does not leave a wounded animal in the bush, it must be hunted down and put out of its misery.

He found a blood spatter and proceeded to track the buffalo. What he did not know at that time was that the most dangerous animal in the bush is a wounded buffalo. He would have known this if he'd *read Jock Of The Bushveld*. The book describes an incident of this nature.

A wounded buffalo, being hunted, will actually circle around and hunt the hunter. This is what makes it so dangerous. People have been killed because of this. Having said this, he was still aware that this was a dangerous animal. It has some mean horns and its sheer size and weight are formidable.

He started tracking it at the site where it was hit. This was difficult at first because of the large number of buffalo spoor. However, scouting around he spotted some blood on the tall grass. Searching further, he found more blood on the leaves of a bush. Tracking was easier after that. Going slowly, he continued tracking, keeping an eye out in front for a possible charge from the beast.

So he was surprised when he heard a crashing of brush from behind him, accompanied by a snort and a roar. He felt the ground tremble as the buffalo charged him. His reflexes were good and he instinctively dived to the side to prevent being trampled to death. As he did so, the buffalo side-swiped at him with its curved horns. This action caused the tip of one horn to slice open the skin on the inside of his upper arm. He was lucky – an inch closer and it would have ripped open a vein. That would have created a potentially fatal situation for Tom.

However, he was still in great danger now as the buffalo had skidded to a halt and was turning around for another charge. He looked around quickly for a place to find safety. There was a tree a few metres away and he headed for it as fast as he could. He determined that he would not have enough time to climb to safety.

He saw that the roots around the tree were above the ground and that there was a hollow under them, probably dug out by a jackal, which would put him out of reach of the animal. Throwing the rifle down, he dived into the hollow, pulling his legs in just in time.

The buffalo, angry, very angry, swung his head and horns at the roots behind which Tom now lay. The big beast continued to try to gore him, even going on its knees to try to get closer. This carried on for what seemed like an eternity. It then seemed to tire and stopped trying to get at Tom.

Taking a few steps back, the buffalo sniffed at the rifle and then proceeded to butt it. Not seeming to be satisfied with this, it trampled all over the rifle. The buffalo again attempted to get at Tom with its horns but gave up after a few tries. Tom recognised that the buffalo's wound was not a fatal one, and there wasn't a lot of blood, so would probably not go down.

He wondered how long the buffalo would hang around trying to get at him. However, shortly after, it snorted, and turned away. Lifting its head high and it tail straight up, it trotted off out of sight.

Tom waited a long time before emerging from under the tree, making sure that the buffalo had gone. He went to pick up the rifle and saw that the butt had been split and broken off, the scope was smashed, and the barrel was bent. "Scratch one rifle", he thought.

He tied a handkerchief around his arm and trudged off back to camp, feeling vulnerable with no rifle.

I'm sure that Tom would remember this vividly for the rest of his life. It's the stuff nightmares are made of.

17 Interesting Driving

Driving to and from Fife was mostly rather boring. Mainly because it was always dark when we travelled and couldn't see any of the countryside.

On one of our trips, however, we did have an exciting incident.

We were on the last strip of dirt road before we would turn onto the access road to the camp. We spotted an impala about to cross the road ahead of us. It hesitated for a moment, then shot forward right in front of us. Rupert swerved the car, which was not a good idea as we were pulling a little trailer. The car started to swing sideways and Rupert struggled to get the slide under control. The impala however was heading on and, just before it was about to be struck by the car, jumped right over the bonnet (hood, to North Americans).

I didn't see which way it went after that but it disappeared from sight. Rupert was still struggling to get control, which he did with great skill. Once the car was stable, someone said "Whew, we were lucky to have missed the impala". Rupert said "What do you mean 'lucky', I was trying to hit the damn thing"!

A memorable incident occurred also while driving into Fife. There was an impala ahead on the side of the road. Tom was driving, Rupert was in the passenger seat (left-hand side in this country), with a rifle. He told Tom not to stop, as the impala would bolt if he did. He leaned out the window and had to take a left-hand shot. He got the impala with a headshot. Left-handed, moving, and a head-shot! That was quite something.

One of the drives to Fife was more interesting. We were travelling with Rupert's father (I don't remember why). He had lived in and around the Lowveld most of his life and would tell us about the history of some of the towns and villages that we drove past, and the prominent people who founded them or had influenced their development. He spoke for hours and we found it quite fascinating.

For example, talking about Sabie: Because the area had always been malaria-free, pioneers in the early days used the area for setting up base camps when hunting and exploring down into the Lowveld. The local Shangaan people called the river "uluSaba" - "the river of fear" because the river was often in flood and teemed with crocodiles. The town got its name from this word. In the 1880s, some farmer lined up a few bottles to use as target practice. The bullets chipped the rock and exposed gold bearing reef. This started a gold-rush into the area and this started the town of Sabie. Needing firewood and timber for mine props, the demand for wood was the start of the huge timber industry in the area around Sabie. Today, Sabie is surrounded by one of the world's largest man-made forests.

The town of Bushbuck Ridge was so named because of the large herds of bushbuck found there in the 1880s. Originally known as Mapulaneng, it has been home to the Mapulana people for centuries. The Mapulana successfully defended the area from Swazi armies who they annihilated at the battle of Moholoholo in 1864.

I won't bore you with the histories of other towns. But, to me, it was fascinating at the time.

He also told interesting hunting stories but, unfortunately, I don't remember any of them.

There was another occasion when we were driving back home, Bunny desperately needed to pee. It was dark and Rupert pulled up on the side of the road. Bunny got out of the car and we saw him walk around to the other side. Then, he disappeared.

I thought it was sort of strange, but dismissed it from my mind. We waited for a minute or two, expecting him to get back in the car. After another couple of minutes, we thought he was taking too long and may be having some trouble.

We got out , and looked to the side but didn't see him. We called his name and heard a muffled reply. Taking a torch, exiting the car, we shone in the direction of the sound. Then we saw that there was a deep ditch next to the road and he had stepped right into it. We pulled him out, with difficulty and, luckily, he was not injured.

18 Epilogue

In looking back at this exciting time of my life, I cherish these memories. I often wished that I could have had more time in the bush.

I was also a little disappointed with my visits to Fife: all the animals of the Lowveld migrated through the property but, in all the times I was there I never saw any of the big five – elephant, rhino, lion, buffalo, and leopard, even though they were in the area. Also, because there were no large bodies of water, there were no hippos or crocodiles.

These were not my only experiences of the bushveld. I had subsequently visited the Kruger National Park but the experience was nowhere near the same. Having to remain in a vehicle was not comparable to wandering around on foot. I visited other game parks closer to home, including Pilanesberg, near Sun City, where my dad was a part-time game ranger (he also farmed ostriches), but it just didn't do it for me.

However, my philosophy has changed somewhat in that I cannot now be a hunter – I cannot bear the thought of killing animals. I can't even kill a fly or an ant. This doesn't mean that I am against hunting. I have no objection to those who hunt for food. I cannot, however condone those that hunt for trophies, or for those who want to kill as many different animals as they can (there are many people like that). I would still like to spend time in the bush because it's a unique experience.

If you found this book of interest, try reading *Jock of the Bushveld* by James Percy FitzPatrick. In addition, read *South African Eden* by James Stevenson-Hamilton, about the founding of the Kruger National

Park. Also try *Memories Of A Game Ranger* by Harry Wolhuter. He was one of the first game rangers of the Kruger National Park. The description of his experience of being brought down by a lion is quite something.

I hope that this little reminiscence of mine has been of interest or entertainment to you, and that you can experience the South African bushveld on foot. It is something that you will never forget.

———————————

ABOUT THE AUTHOR

Robert V Lund was born in Johannesburg, South Africa and spent the first forty-three years of his life there before moving to Toronto, Canada, with his family. He has published several books relating to spirituality, and the Masonic fraternity.

www.ingramcontent.com/pod-product-compliance
Lightning Source LLC
Chambersburg PA
CBHW070028260726
48658CB00002B/548